Journeys Of Change

Written by Felicia Thompson

Published by

Written Inspired Publishing

Written Inspired Publishing
PO Box 92265
Washington, DC 20090
writteninspired@comcast.net

Journeys of Change
Copyright ©2010 Felicia Thompson

All Written Inspired Publishing books may be purchased for education, business or sales promotional use. For information, please write: Special Markets Department, Written Inspired Publishing, P. O. Box 92265, Washington, DC 20090.

All poems are original works by the author.

Library of Congress Control Number: 2010941173

ISBN-13: 978-0-615-41223-8
ISBN-10: 0615412238

Printed in the United States of America

*I dedicate this book
to my baby girl,
Danyielle*

Table of Contents

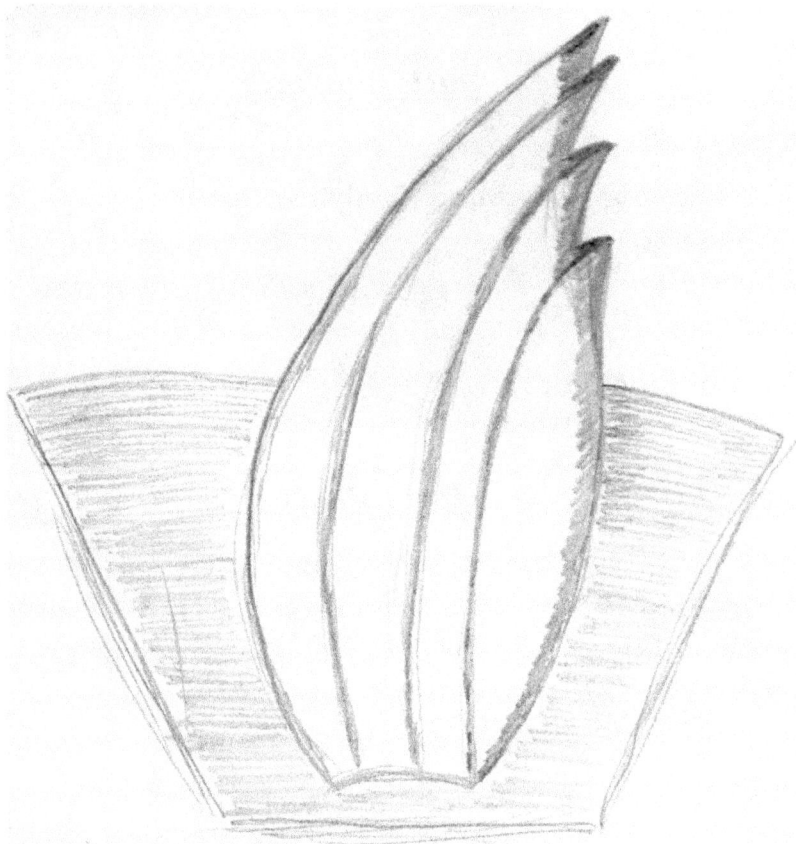

Acknowledgments

I want to thank my family and friends for their support in writing this book.

I want to thank Pastor Deron & Jill Cloud for being life coaches and living a transparent life. I want to thank them for being a model of confidence, strength, passion and love. I want to thank them for being generous in all of their talents: speaking, sharing, advising, teaching and inspiring.

I want to thank my family for their support, from encouragement to babysitting, sharing a word, changing my perspective on a situation or just an expression of love.

Introduction

Life is your experience and your reactions. This is an adventure that you take daily. Your decisions are based on what you have learned and seen throughout your life. The people who were and are involved in your life influence the way you live your life. Those influences impact what you like and don't like. What you like and don't like determines your present and future.

My journey began with the way my parents were raised, how they were influenced, the advice they followed, and what they believed. My parents taught me what they knew. My surroundings and environment were also important in my life. The things around me are an influence on how I think and what I perceive to be normal or abnormal.

My experiences guided me through life as a teenager into adulthood. Life means changes. Sometimes it's difficult learning new things but when you make adjustments to the changes you move forward. Do I have a model? Do I know what is best to add in my life? Do I know what to take out to move on with life? It becomes a learning and growing process as I move forward in life.

As I began my journey, the next five chapters have helped me get through. Read each chapter and see if it helps you through your daily walk. These words have been formulated through conversations I have had with my Creator.

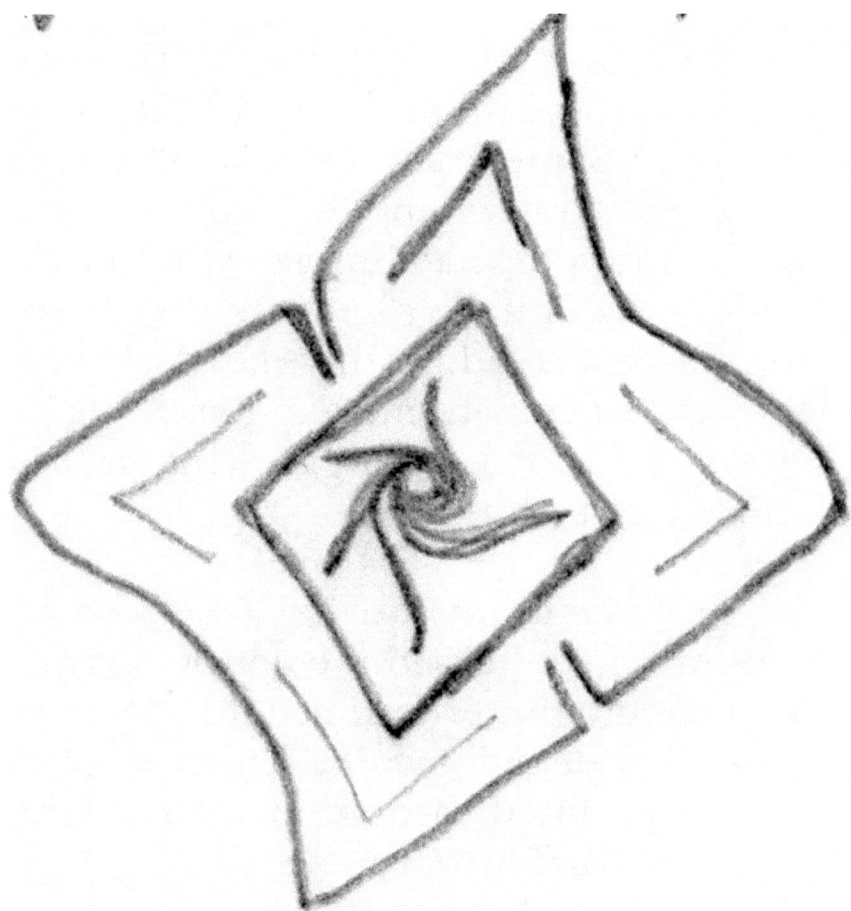

Chapter 1   Creating You

Becoming a person of value from the influences around you. What you learn and choose to live by is important to how you will function in society.

Functioning in society is on a daily "basis" learning something new or a refresher to become a member of the community. Give back to society what society has given to you.

Personality Bank

A bank that is filled from many different sources,
The influences all around you is
how you start out being you.
From parents, teachers, coaches and friends,
Each one deposits something different in the
bank.
From colors, to smells, to taste, to manners
Whatever is deposited will be good or bad and will
either make you grow or stagnant you.
Everything comes with a different perspective
Cultures and environments are your most
prominent influence.
Forced or willing all is taken in.
Living and acting shows what was retained.
What is learned?
What is lived?
What is said is deep within the heart.
As the bank takes it in
It continues to grow and continues to expand.
As things are continuously deposited in the bank,
It continues to build.
Withdrawals are always taken and
Deposits are always made.
What's important about withdrawals from the
bank is what you do with the withdrawal.
How you use those withdrawals
will either help or hinder.

Growing Into Me

Knowing about me is
finding out what I want.
Knowing about me is
finding out what I like to do.
Knowing about me is
doing different things.
Knowing about me is
acknowledging my feelings honestly.
Knowing about me is
being able to help other people.
Knowing about me is
being able to deal with different people
and not lose me in the process.
Knowing about me is
being honest about the different activities
that I like to try.
To grow into me, I have to experience different
things to find out what I like and what I need.

Education

Education forms how you live your life.
Your life consists of what you know.
It walks hand in hand with growth.
Reading increases your knowledge.
Your knowledge will help you understand.
Your understanding makes your growth powerful.
The growth is powerful for your walk.
Your walk determines your path.
Your path takes you to your future
and knowledge.
When you increase your knowledge,
You make a powerful choice.

You reach your future with education either by
force or willingness.

Reading associated with your understanding
which leads to your action that will determine
your growth and what path you take.

Understanding will determine your path.
Your action will be guided by your understanding.
Your action will display your growth.

Listening

I heard the message and didn't fall asleep.
I decided to focus on the message and
not the delivery.
I got more out of it than I thought I would.

I can help instead of hindering.
I can progress instead of diminishing.
I can give instead of taking.
I can accomplish all of this because
I Listened!

Journey Traveled

A journey worth traveling, you take.
A journey worth having, you do.
A journey worth fighting, you fight.
A journey worth building, you build on.
A journey to grow in, you stay in.
A journey to grow from, you apply it.
A journey you build from, it's what you put in it.

What you take in, you make it your own.
That journey will mold you.
That journey is where you will live.
Your journey presents a new set of circumstances
to build on.
Each journey you learn from, you teach from by
passing it on.

Chapter 2   Becoming You

Living what you have learned both good and bad. Not always having consideration for others. Showing society what they taught you as they poured into your life in many different forms.

I'm Into Me

I don't want to do this anymore.
I see no growth.
I see no point.

I don't stop to think about what is going on
because I don't want to care.
I don't want to make the effort to make the change.
I don't like what I have to do.
I choose to not make things happen.

It feels better to complain.
In my world complaining gets me through.
It gives me the excuse not to do the things that I
need to do.

See Me

I want you to see me through my eyes.
I want you to see me and smile.
I want you to feel what I feel.

I want you to enjoy me.
I want you to enjoy my touch.
I want you to enjoy my sound.
I want you to enjoy my words.
I want you to enjoy my time.

I want to love you for all you do.
I want to love you for your style.
I want to love you for your touch.
I want to love you for your sound.
I want to love you for your words.
I want to love you because you are you.

I want to love you because I can trust you.
I want to love you because you are real.
I want to love you because I choose to.

The Mask

The mask that hides me or
so I thought.
The mask shows the world something other than
my thoughts.
The mask that gave me a false sense of hope.
It is there so that you move on about your journey.
I don't want you to see who I am because it does
not fit what you think of me.
This mask has me doing things that
I am not ready to be.
When placed in different circumstances,
the mask does not reveal the true me.
To be able to be free from the mask
that holds on to me.
To reveal the parts of me that I try to hide
from you so you won't see,
The mask is what I wear,
so I don't have to be me.

Prison

Stuck in a time and place where there is
hopelessness and pain.
In a box with no way out.
In a world that has no support.
A space that causes pain and you have no control.
A place that has no time for appeal.

In the dark where things are revealed,
No sight to look ahead.
A place where punishment begins and luxuries are
taken away.
Taking your right to choose and use.

A place that will slow you down.
A place that will change your future.
A place where you cannot express yourself.
Not free to be who you are.
Experiencing an unwanted lesson.
Trying to survive the pain of the adversity.

Shadows

Hiding in the shadows of my pain:
> I show you a façade of happiness,
> I tried to give you a softer side of me,
> I accept that state of being,
> I accept the unhappiness as my norm,
> I decide my future,
> I make or break my dream,
> I work hard to stay above water.

Little did I know that the shadows showed the pain, discomfort and unhappiness.
It showed everything that I tried to hide inside.
It showed the most uncomfortable thing of all, it showed the wall that I had been hiding behind.

Struggles

When you are scared,
your Father gives courage.
When you are weak,
He gives you strength.
When you feel you have nothing to look forward to,
He gives a vision.
When you have no aspiration,
He gives you goals.
When you lose sight of your goals,
He will focus you.
When you feel you do not have what it takes to reach
your goals, He gives you everything you need.
When you shy away, He gives you boldness.
When you are unable to know who is good and who
means you no good, He gives you
the gift of discernment.
When you feel you cannot express your feelings,
He gives you the ability to communicate.
When you feel low, He can lift you up.
When you think you are ugly,
He shows you, you are beautiful.
When you think things are not right,
He works them out for your good.
He gives you gifts
It's up to you to discover what they are
It's up to you to learn how to use them and sharing
it can benefit others.

Losing Track

I had something to accomplish
but before I could complete the task,
I started something else.
A bunch of steps needed to be made
but spent too much time on one step,
could not get to the rest to complete the task.

I lost track of time to accomplish the mission
when I lost focus of my tasks.
I lost track of my passion
when I engaged in others actions.
I could not walk in the mission
because I allowed others to dictate the functions of
my actions.

I lost track of my vision
When I focused on others agendas,
on others problems, on others goals,
and the mission is never reached.

I lost track of the next step
that needed to be achieved.
I'm so busy helping others
that I had run out of time to reach my goals.

Carrying others slack
when the ball had been dropped,
I missed an opportunity.

When I lost track to make it back
I started one step,
Thought of something else
spent more time than I should have and the step
had to be started all over again, because I lost
track of my mission.

Emptiness In My Actions

Why does it bother me so much
that I have become one with you?
No emotions have been put into the connection
that we created as two.
Even though we shared an open door policy,
a straight forward relationship performing an act
of oneness complicated our everything.

How I walk as a person,
how I walk as a leader,
how I lead in my home has been compromised.
Compromise became a main factor in my home and
interrupted my life.
It hurt to feel the way I do
not having what I wanted.
It hurt to know that it was going to happen.
I did not listen to the response in my heart.
It hurt to know that I did not get
all of what I wanted.

Opening up my heart to an emptiness in my
actions.
Opening up my heart to building ties
that does not have meaning.
Opening up my heart to a change in the
relationship.

How do I continue to build a relationship?
How do I continue to move forward?

I feel I have let them get to close to me.
How do I move forward?
I feel a void in our actions.
How do I move forward?
We have made clear that this will not be something
done on a regular.

How do I give what I don't have?
How do I get what I think I want?
How do we pick up from where we where before the
emptiness became a part of our relationship?
How do you move forward when you have committed
your body to another?
How do I give to someone else
what I have given to you?
How do you take lightly the connecting of two?
How do you take lightly the emptiness that the person
has passed to you?
How do you have a meaningful relationship that had
not been built with a strong foundation?
Having stuff in common does not build what is needed
but fosters that connection.
Having stuff that you can do together makes the tie
longer and stronger.

We connected on a false building.
We connected on a weak bond.
We connected leaving a stretched string to break and
not a thick knot.
The door has been open to continue receiving the
empty actions that we committed.
The door has been open to receive empty promises.
The door has been open to feel the abundance of pain.
The Emptiness in my Actions!

Chapter 3   Exposed

What have you been doing and who are you as a person? It's about what you have learned, what you are seeing, how you are living, what you are experiencing has taken over your life. Some things are good and some are bad. Some things have altered your life and how you will continue to live your life. It's about being shown what's right and what's wrong and choosing to do something about it.

Exposed

Being exposed is something
I don't pay attention to.
Don't care about the consequences
until it's too late.
Exposure opens the doors to many things.
I'm exposed by both the good and bad.
How I choose to look at the exposure
is most important.

Being exposed shows what I've contemplated.
Being exposed will make me admit my mistakes.
Being exposed makes me correct the wrong.

Being exposed will open my eyes.
Being exposed presents many opportunities.
Being exposed gives me different perspectives.
Being exposed will help me grow.
Being exposed will illustrate where I could go and
what I can do.

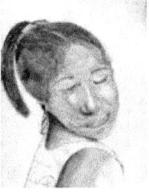

Closing My Eyes

When I close my eyes,
what do I see glimpses of my past chasing after me.
When I close my eyes,
where do I wonder, in a place of pleasing me.
When I close my eyes where do I go,
to a place of rest.
When I close my eyes,
I run to escape the pressure of my life
When I close my eyes,
what do I see,
what I want to become when my eyes open again.
When I close my eyes,
what do I see, an opportunity to shut out all the
distractions competing for me.
When I close my eyes,
I find myself resting to replenish me.
When I close my eyes, I close them to take a pause
before taking my next step.
When I close my eyes,
I have a bunch of things happening to me and then
I open them to act on the things I've experienced.
When I close my eyes I believe I have escaped only
to find the things are still out there waiting on me
to face reality.

<u>Rules</u>

You live by what you've been taught.
You walk by what you see.
You talk by what you hear.
You are what has been driven into you.
You have been given a set of principles to use daily.
Many have not been written but followed.
Do you just live by it or do you question its validity.
For years you have been living according to your
instincts to survive.

When you become of age, you look at what you do
and question if this is what you should do.
Does it really make sense?
Does it help you spiritually?
What tactics are you considering?
What approach do you take?

Prepare yourself by making a roadmap.
Know what to live by and if adjustments need to be
made, do it.
Layout what you know and believe in.
Evaluate the reasoning behind what you know
and believe.
Once you have laid out and evaluated what you
know and believe,
Formulate your guidelines and live by them
Both written and unwritten.

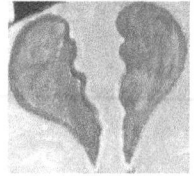

Broken But Not Giving Up

Been taken advantage of,
left in a bind left behind,
But I'm moving forward and not giving up.
Been driven to drink, been talked about, been
misused and abused,
But I'm moving forward and not giving up.

Been taken from, been misplaced, been looked over
and ignored,
But I'm moving forward and not giving up.
Ideas dismissed, possessions taken, paths with
obstacles after obstacles,
But I'm moving forward and not giving up.
Been distracted, been confused, been disappointed,
But I'm learning, moving forward and
not giving up.

See what you see,
Learn from what you have experienced,
Understand how you use your experiences to help
another person.
Move forward and not give up
Unsure of self, nerves about different situations,
afraid to make a change
But I'm still moving forward and not giving up.

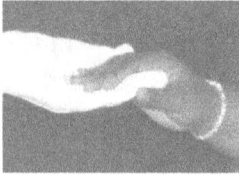

Holding My Hand

Holding my hand to:
Show me affection,
Show me direction,
Give me advice,
Give me correction,
Be my friend,
Be friendly,
Comfort me,
Show me closeness,
Display what I mean to you,
Show that you trust me,
Show the connection that we have,
Pull me closer to you,
Display a little romantic move,
Show that you are true,
Show a loving embrace,
Give claim to what you want,
Smooth out a major wrong.

My Connection with You

Is important to me because:
>You carry and lift me,
>You build and encourage me,
>You lead and guide me,
>You protect and nurture my soul,
>You make me whole and mend my heart,
>You look after me in the dark and love me in the mist,
>You shelter me in the storm and walk with me through it all,
>You gave me your best and did not treat me like the rest,
>You showed me what I like and help me get my life back,
>You told me what I needed to hear and listen to me to help me get rid of the fear,
>You showed me what love is and how it would be if I shared it with all in need.

All I need and want is to continue my journey as I grow in my connection with you.

Future Positioning

I'm looking to better my life.
Write down my ideas.
Work on steps to build that idea.
Search high and low for those who
have come close.
Look to see where others slow down
or cause me to stumble.
Make adjustments in my life accordingly.
Get rid of any objections that
do not support my goals.
Work through any obstacles that surface.
Step on the stones to reach the stars.
Work hard with others to make it happen.
I will continue to work on my future positioning.

Positioning

Where I see myself is my decision.
Where I want to be is my choice.
Where I like to be is up to me.
I must choose where I want to be.
I must choose how I get there through opportunity.
I must carefully plan each path I take.
I must do what it takes.
I have to decide to stay focused.
I have to decide to take action when needed.
Where I go is an attitude.
I have to arrange the time and
each step that I take.
I chose to be where I am.

Pruning

How many have been pruned?
How many go through the process of getting stuff off
of them?
How many see the things that they have to give up and
decide to walk away.
Walk away because the very thing that is being removed
is what keeps them moving.
How many times do you go through something you think
you have gotten rid of just to find you have only gone
through one step and there are many more steps to go.
How many times will you hold on to things that stop you
from growing because it is comfortable?
How many times will you walk away from a situation to
find out that you have to go through that situation to go
to where you want to be dreading the fact that its your
goal because you have to take the path to reach your
final destination?
How do you love and accept pruning?
How do you overlook what it takes to make
things happen?
How do you overlook having to go through situations you
don't like?
Think about the destination.
Think about the benefits you will receive.
Think about who you will help.
Think about where you could go.
Think about how you will affect others.

Think about where you want to go, what you want
to experience,
How you want to experience,
How much you want to experience,
It is a hard experience but a great reward.

Alterations

When you make changes in clothing,
you make adjustments to your image.
When you change your attitude,
you make adjustments to your character.
When you change who you hang with,
you make adjustments to experience different things.
When you change your way of thinking,
you make adjustments to your way of living.
When you change your reading habits,
you make adjustments to your knowledge.
When you change your language,
you make adjustments to the many opportunities you
get to experience.
When you change your life
you make adjustments that will help you grow.

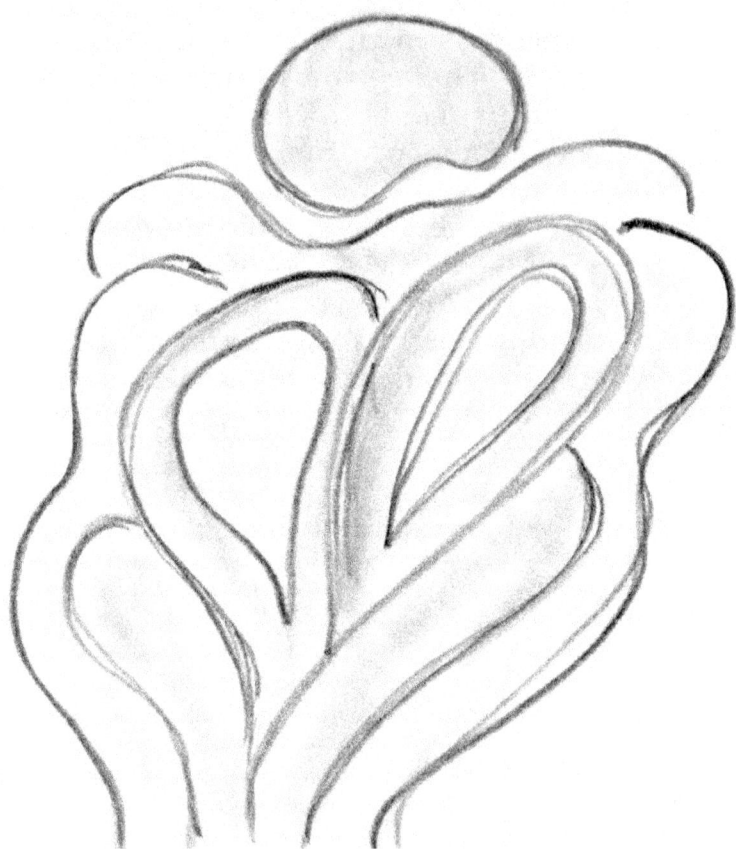

Chapter 4   Building You

After deciding what needs to be changed, what needs to be worked on, you begin to correct it, build it, nurture it and Love you. You begin to know how you will live changed. You will begin to form new practices and treat them like habits.

New Management

Why we don't succeed?
We don't know who we are.
Why we don't elevate?
We don't know who we are.
Why we don't complete our mission?
We don't know who we are.

Our life is a mess because we don't know
who we are.
We end up in unhealthy relationships because we
don't know who we are.
We walk in other people's vision for our life
because we don't know who we are.
We blame our mistakes and choices on others
because we don't know who we are.

Who are we?
      We are people of Love.
      We are people of talents.
      We are people of many opportunities.
      We are a people of authority.

Especially when we walk in His word, His love and
His guidance by way of the word.
Then we will know who we are.

Develop Your Mind, Body & Soul

Discovering what you want becomes a challenge
Forming a plan is the most important task
Organizing the ideas is the next step to building you
Strategizing becomes your friend
The strategies foster your steps
Establishing those steps should link up with what you want to build
Building your knowledge helps you to figure out life's questions

Building your body
  Define what you want it to be
  Develop your health through shaping your muscles,
  Customize your food plan and exercise routines

Building your spirit
  Taking the time to read spiritual literature
  Meditate on what you have read
  Find out how to implement in your daily life
  After figuring out how you implement,
  you just do it
  Taking the time to share with others

Building your mind
  Experience different things and go to different place
  See different things, hear different things, and read different things
  Be involved in different things at least once
  Look at how it can or will enhance you

Look at how you can incorporate it in your daily life or even build on it

Building You

Building you is finding out what you like and what
you want for your life.
Building you is finding out what it takes to make you
what you want to be.
Building you is making the necessary steps to be
what you want and not let anyone change your mind.

Building you is evaluating your mind,
body and soul.
Decide what you like and don't like.
Determine how you can benefit someone else with
the change that you make with you.

Building you, you have to visualize the change.
You then need to elaborate on the change.
You then need to assemble those changes,
implementing them one by one.
You build a new you for someone behind you.
How you build the new you is all in the technique
that you choose to make that new you.

Building A House

Are you using the nails to hold the wood together
or are you using the Father's word to hold your
house together?

Are you using the wood to build the frame or are
you using His word to build your lifestyle?
Are you using the paint to make the outside look
pretty or are you building your character that
makes your outside look pretty?
Are you adding furniture to fill your home or are
you filing your house with the word for Him to fill
your home?

Many of us look at our home as a place of rest,
entertainment and comfort.
Many others look at it as a place of service where
you serve others.
You share with others.
You love others.
You give to others.

When you build your home you are able to love
others in spite of right or wrong.
Reveal an alternative way when lost, serve others
among you and give unconditionally.

Communicating

How we talk to one another is key to everything.
How we interact with each other,
A soft touch with your hand,
A gentle kiss from the lips,
An ear to hear your thoughts,
A heart for understanding.

A word to encourage,
An action to ignite the fire in your step,
A nudge to help you move forward.
A showing of support through your actions.

Build a connection to constantly work to a goal.
Connecting with each other through
time and space.
A few gestures to touch the Soul
That's communicating!

Investing

In order to survive you must invest.
You must invest in you as a person of value.
You must invest in yourself to move forward.
It is what helps to shape your choices,
opportunities and life.

Knowing what excites helps direct your path.
In order to grow in the path, first look at all aspects
of that excitement.
See what it will take to make it a skill.

Decide whether or not to put the effort into what
you are looking at to make it a part of your life.

Continue to research it to find out what paths it
can take you.
Find out How much money is needed to fund that
skill.

What will it take to get started?
What will it take to fund continuous education?
What is the best way to continue your education?
How can you use that skill to assist another
person?
How can that skill be use to better someone else's
life?
Can someone else be persuaded to get the same
skills from the excitement displayed?

Must be able to visualize the skill.
Must live and breathe it.
Must know how to market this skill to others not
only to buy into it but also to learn from it and
enjoy it.

Investing now means building for the future.
It means building a legacy.
It means bringing a change to someone else's life.
Being able to help someone with a need because I
invested in me.

Being able to love life because I made a choice to
put more into me through words, music, reading,
learning, meditating, listening and being selective.

Branching Out

Seeing something and going after it.
Looking at what's involved and figuring it out.
Being in the present using your gifts and talents.
Living and planning for the future.
Loving self so that you're able to help someone else.
When you give in one aspect, you receive in many others.

Making an Investment

How do I get ahead?
I have to look where I'm going.
How do I build who I am?
I have to continuously feed my mind through
reading, meditation and understanding.
How do I develop me?
I continue to improve what I know, I make it
my own, I add to what I understand.
How do I move to another level?
Working with others as well as independently
with steps that take me where I want to go.

Chapter 5   Living Changed

Once you have made a change, you continue to live the changes that you have made and not go back to what you have decided to get rid of. Some of your actions that you were living before were not working for you.

Be an Example

What you do, someone is looking.
What you say, someone is listening.
How you act, someone is constantly watching.
Where you go, people will follow.
What you allow,
helps people to decide whether or
not to follow you.

People look at you and act on your actions.
People determine your character
by your actions.
People determine your knowledge by what you
prove that you know when you talk about
what you know.
People adjust themselves according to you
how you act or how you are
perceived by others.

Freedom

Freedom to live
Freedom to speak
Freedom to walk
Freedom to dance
Freedom to have
Freedom to give
Freedom to help
Freedom to write
Freedom to create
Freedom to listen
Freedom to choose
Freedom to act
Freedom to show
Freedom to dare
Freedom to challenge.

Unconditional

Having no limits.
Having an abundance to give.
Giving with no expectation to receive.
Using your resources with no limits on how you
use them or who you use them for.

Having a lifetime to build.
Building the things that are given to you.
Building will never end as long as you
continue to feed.

Once you stop feeding you slow down
When you slow down you become stagnant
When you become stagnant you lose out on
what's ahead
What's ahead will save your life

Don't become stagnant for it will make you
become conditional
Conditional will stop you from experiencing,
expanding and learning more of what
will move you forward.

Lets Party

Are you partying to escape, have fun or
network?
When you party does it add or take value away
from your life?
Are you choosing what type of party you go to?
Are you monitoring your conduct or going with
the flow?
Are you participating in what's going on or are
you going against the majority?
Does this party put your life in jeopardy?
Are you taking away from others or
Are you adding value to someone else's life at
this party?

When you party know who you are
partying with.
Know why you are partying with them.
Know what you will give and what you expect to
receive from the party.
Don't just party to have fun but party to learn,
to celebrate and to advance someone else.

Building Me Continuously

I find a place of peace.
A place to retreat.
A place without distraction.
A place to look deep into my mind.
A place to listen to my heart.
A place to hear my thoughts.
A place to embrace my environments.

I take time to build my knowledge and skills.
A time to build my confidence.
A time to build my worth.
A time to be able to plan and create.
A time to invent and produce.
A time to communicate.
A time to grow and help others.
A time to build my opinion.
Time to continuously build ME!

Investing For Life

You have to constantly put into yourself.
You have to often move or you will get stuck.
You have to set goals, a vision and aspirations.
You have to constantly read,
understand and apply in order to survive.
You have to occasionally take time for yourself.
You have to give constantly to help not only
yourself but others as well.

Marketing

Know who you are.
Know your objective (mission).
Know what you stand for.
Know what you provide.
Know your niche and be able to talk about it.
Know how you add value to another.
Know how to increase your knowledge and
make it happen.
Know what makes you unique.
Creativity needs to always be used in reaching
your objective.
Know how to make yourself stand out.
Know how to leave something for others to
remember you by.
Build strategies to reach your objective.
Use the tactics created in your strategies.
Meet your deadlines.
If you miss the deadline then create a new one
and make every effort to reach your goal.

Topic Index

Afterword

I hope you enjoyed Journeys of Change. You have read about some of my experiences and I hope you were inspired by my poems and drawings.

If you have purchased this poetry collection, thank you for your support. If you have borrowed this book to read for your personal enjoyment, thank you for interest. Either way, share with a friend.

Sincerely,

Felicia Thompson
Poet & Author

Share your thoughts with me by sending an email to
<u>writteninspired@comcast.net</u>

To schedule Felicia Thompson for signings, book events, book club discussions, or poetry readings, please contact:

Written Inspired Publishing
(202)277-5172

Visit my website:

<u>http://www.writteninspiredpub.com/</u>

www.ingramcontent.com/pod-product-compliance
Lightning Source LLC
LaVergne TN
LVHW051710080426
835511LV00017B/2830